THE **TESTING** SERIES

PO! ICE SPECIAL CONSTABLE INTERVIEW

QUESTIONS & ANSWERS

THE **TESTING** SERIES
expert advice on test preparation

how2become

Orders: Please contact How2become Ltd, Suite 2, 50 Churchill Square Business Centre, Kings Hill, Kent ME19 4YU.
You can also order via the e mail address info@how2become.co.uk.

ISBN: 9781907558320

First published 2012

Typeset for How2become Ltd by Molly Hill, Canada.

Printed in Great Britain for How2become Ltd by Bell & Bain Ltd, 303 Burnfield Road, Thornliebank, Glasgow G46 7UQ.

INTRODUCTION

Welcome to your new guide, **Police Special Constable Interview Questions and Answers**. This guide has been designed to help you prepare for and pass the police special constable interview in England and Wales. The questions and answers contained within this guide are relevant for both the assessment centre interview and the final interview (if applicable). The final interview may not be applicable to the Police Force you are applying to join, so please check before using the questions in your preparation.

The selection process to join the police as a special constable is highly competitive. Armed with this insider's guide, you have certainly taken the first step to passing the interview for becoming a police special constable.

The guide contains a large number of sample interview questions and answers which are designed to make it easier for you to prepare. Read the questions and answers carefully and take notes as you progress. It is important to point out at the early stage that you should not copy the examples provided in the answers to the questions, but alternatively use them as a basis for your own preparation. It is essential that you provide responses to the questions that are based on your own individual experiences.

Don't ever give up on your dreams; if you really want to become a police special constable then you can do it. The way to approach the interview is to embark on a programme of 'in-depth' preparation, and this guide will show you exactly how to do that.

The way to pass the police special constable interview is to develop your own skills and experiences around the core competencies that are required for the role. You should also aim to provide as much 'evidence' as possible when responding to the questions. Many candidates who apply to join the police will be unaware that the core competencies even exist. As you progress through this guide you will find that these important elements of the police specials role will form the foundations of your preparation. So, the first step in your preparation, and before we go any further, is to get hold of a copy of the police special constable core competencies. They will usually form part of your application pack but if they don't, you can obtain a copy of them by visiting the website of the force you are applying to join.

If you need any further help with any elements of the selection process, including role play, written test and interview, then we offer a wide range of products to assist you. These are all available through our online shop www.how2become.co.uk.

Once again, thank you for your custom and we wish you every success in your pursuit to becoming a police officer.

Work hard, stay focused and be what you want...

Best wishes,

The how2become team

The How2become Team

PREFACE BY AUTHOR RICHARD MCMUNN

In 1993 I joined the Fire Service after serving four years in the Fleet Air Arm branch of the Royal Navy. After spending 16 successful years in the Fire Service, I decided to set up my own business and teach people like you how to prepare for a specific job. I have passed many different job applications and interviews during my life and I have also sat on the opposite side of the interview desk. Therefore, I have plenty of experience and knowledge that I will be sharing with you throughout this guide.

Throughout my career and working life I have always found that if I apply myself, and focus on the job in hand, then I will be successful. It is a formula that I have stuck with for many years and it has always served me well. This kind of approach is one that I want to teach you over the forthcoming pages of this guide and I hope that you will use my skills and knowledge to help you achieve the same levels of success that I have enjoyed.

Personally, I do not believe in luck when applying for jobs. I believe those candidates who successfully pass the police officer selection process do so because they thoroughly deserve it. They have prepared well and they have worked hard in order to improve their skills and knowledge.

I have always been a great believer in preparation. Preparation was my key to success and it is also yours. Without the right level of preparation you will be setting out on the route to failure. The Police Service is hard to join, but if you follow the steps that I have compiled within this guide then you will increase your chances of success dramatically. Remember, you are learning how to be a successful candidate, not a successful police special constable.

The Police Force, like many other public services, has changed a great deal over the years and even more so in how it assesses potential candidates for police officer positions. The men and women of the UK Police Force carry out an amazing job. They are there to protect the community in which they serve and they do that job with great pride, passion and very high levels of professionalism and commitment. They are to be congratulated for the service they provide.

HOW TO PASS THE POLICE SPECIAL CONSTABLE INTERVIEW

Passing the interview is relatively easy. Here's how to pass it:

STEP 1 – LEARN THE CORE COMPETENCIES RELEVANT TO THE ROLE

If you fail to learn the core competencies that are relevant to the role of a police special then you will more than likely fail. Your first step is to obtain a copy of these important attributes. Once you have a copy, you must read them, learn them and be able to provide evidence of where you match each and every one of them.

Anybody can go to an interview and tell the panel that would be a good police special, but actually backing this claim up with evidence is the key to success. The interview panel want to know that you have experience already in key areas, because if you already have experience in these areas, then you are far more likely to perform well in the role.

The core competencies for becoming a police special constable do change from time-to-time. However, at the time of writing, the following core competencies apply:

- Problem Solving

- Respect for Race and Diversity
- Resilience
- Effective Communication
- Team Working
- Customer and Community Focus
- Personal Responsibility

If the core competencies that you are going to be assessed against during your particular interview vary, do not worry; the process that I have provided you within this workbook will help you to pass the interview and provide sufficient evidence to match the core competencies.

STEP 2 – PROVIDE EVIDENCE OF WHERE YOU MEET EVERY ASSESSABLE CORE COMPETENCY

This step is very important, therefore, do not ignore it. When responding to the interview questions that form part of the assessment centre interview, you must provide lots of evidence of where you have already demonstrated the competency being assessed. Let's take a look at a sample police special interview question:

SAMPLE QUESTION

Provide me with an example of where you have been resilient during a difficult and testing situation?

The above question relates to the core competency of confidence and resilience. Now take a look at a sample response:

SAMPLE RESPONSE

"Whilst working as a barman in a previous role I was confronted with a difficult and potentially hostile situation to deal with. It was a Sunday afternoon and a large group of men entered the bar after a local football match had ended. They were a group of traveling fans and their team had just been beaten by the home side. Naturally they were disappointed about the result and they wanted to have a drink before catching their train home. Everything was fine for the first half-hour. However, after a while a number of them started to become verbally abusive to a small number of home

fans who were drinking in another part of the pub. I started off by asking then men to refrain from using such language. I did this in a calm manner and explained that there were families within the pub too and that this kind of behaviour was not welcome. Despite my pleas they continued to use unwelcome language.

I remained calm and approached the men in a non-confrontational manner. I used open body language and spoke in a calm but firm manner. I informed them that I would not serve them anymore drinks and that they must leave immediately. One of the group began to shout at me stating his annoyance at my stance. I warned him that if they did not leave immediately I would call the police.

The men then left the pub and there was no more trouble. I believe it was important to maintain a resilient stance during the situation and to also portray a confident manner. However, I also ensured that I did not come across in an aggressive or confrontational manner as I believe this would have only made the situation worse."

The above response is an excellent answer to the question for the following reasons:

1. It provides actual evidence of a where a person has demonstrated the core competency of **confidence and resilience**.

2. The response is detailed in a logical manner, with a beginning a middle and an end. This is important as you will be assessed against effective communication during the interview.

3. The person remains calm throughout the entire scenario and manages to deal with it in a positive manner with a positive end result.

STEP 3 – USE THE S.T.A.R METHOD WHEN RESPONDING TO THE INTERVIEW QUESTIONS AT ASSESSMENT CENTRE.

The STAR method is one that I have used during my preparation for many interviews in the past. It works most effectively when preparing responses to situational type interview questions. I would certainly recommend that you use it during the police special constable assessment centre interview.

The STAR method basically ensures that your responses to the interview questions follow a concise logical sequence and also that you cover every possible area. Here's a breakdown of what it actually means:

Situation – At the commencement of my response I will explain what the situation was and who else was involved. This will be a relatively comprehensive explanation so that the interviewer fully understands what it is I am trying to explain.

Task – I will then explain what the task was. This will basically be an explanation of what had to be done and by whom.

Action – I will then move on and explain what action I specifically took, and also what action other people took.

Result – I will finally explain what the result was following my actions. It is important to make sure that the result was positive as a result of your actions.

Have a go at using the **STAR** method when creating responses to the sample interview questions that I provide you within this guide. Write down the question at the top of a sheet of paper and write down each individual element underneath it.

STEP 4 – WORK ON YOUR INTERVIEW TECHNIQUE

During your pre-interview preparation, concentrate on developing your interview technique. This will involve concentrating on the following key areas:

- Creating a positive first impression when you walk into the interview room
- Presentation – how you come across to the interview panel
- Effective communication – how your speak and how you construct your responses to the questions
- Body language and posture
- Final questions that you ask at the end of the interview
- Creating a positive final impression

Let's now break down each of these areas and look at them in detail.

CREATING A POSITIVE FIRST IMPRESSION

The police special constable interview panel will naturally create a first impression of you. As soon as you walk into the interview room they will be forming an opinion. Therefore, it is important that you get off on the right foot. Whenever I walk into any interview room I will always follow this process:

Knock before I enter the room

↓

Walk into the interview room standing tall and smiling

↓

Stand by the interview chair and say
"Hello, I'm Richard, pleased to meet you."

↓

Shake the hand of each interviewer firmly, whilst looking them in the eye

↓

Sit down in the interview chair, only when invited to do so

↓

Sit in the interview chair with an upright posture and with my hands resting palms facing downwards on the top of my knees, feet firmly on the floor

By following the above process I will be creating a positive first impression and demonstrating good qualities such as manners, self-discipline, politeness and motivation.

PRESENTATION

Presentation effectively means how you intend to dress for the interview and also how you intend to come across at the interview. You should want the interview panel to see you as a professional, motivated, conscientious and caring person who is taking the interview very seriously. I recommend that you wear a smart and formal outfit for the interview. Make sure that your suit/outfit is cleaned and pressed, your shoes are polished and your personal hygiene is up to standard. You should take into consideration that you are applying to join a disciplined service; therefore, you should portray the image that you are a disciplined and organised person. This means simple things such as taking a shower, shaving, having a haircut and general grooming. You should avoid brightly coloured clothes and generally go for a conservative approach such a dark blue, black or grey suit. I would strongly advise that you avoid brightly coloured socks or ties with cartoon characters on them!

EXAMPLE OF A GOOD APPLICANT

A good applicant is someone who has taken the time to prepare. They have researched both the police force they are applying to join and also the role that they are being interviewed for. They may not know every detail about the police force and the role but it will be clear that they have made an effort to find out important facts and information, such as the core competencies, the geographical area of the force, information relating to current police force activities, local/neighbourhood policing initiatives and firm evidence of where they meet the assessable areas.

They will be well presented at the interview and they will be confident, but not overconfident. As soon as they walk into the interview room they will be polite and courteous and they will sit down in the interview chair only when invited to do so. Throughout the interview they will sit upright in the chair and communicate in a positive manner. Their responses to the questions will be structured in a concise and logical manner. If they do not know the answer to a question they will say so and they won't try to waffle. At the end of the interview they will ask positive questions about the job or the organisation before shaking hands and leaving.

A POOR APPLICANT

A poor applicant could be any combination of the following. They will be late for the interview or even forget to turn up at all. They will have made little effort to dress smartly and they will have carried out little or no preparation. When asked questions about the role they will have little or no knowledge. Throughout the interview they will appear to be unenthusiastic about the whole process and will look as if they want the interview to be over as soon as possible. Whilst sat in the interview chair they will slouch and fidget. At the end of the interview they will try to ask clever questions that are intended to impress the panel.

IMPROVING INTERVIEW TECHNIQUE

How you present yourself during the police special constable interview is important. Whilst assessing candidates for interviews I will not only assess their responses to the interview questions but I will also pay attention to the way they present themselves. A candidate could give excellent responses to the interview questions but if they present themselves in a negative manner then this can lose them marks.

In the build-up to your interview practice a few mock interviews. Look to improve your interview technique as well as working on your responses to the interview questions.

EFFECTIVE COMMUNICATION

Effective communication is all about how you speak to the interview panel and also how you listen to what they have to say.

When responding to the interview questions you should speak clearly and concisely, avoiding all forms of waffle, slang or hesitations such as 'erm'. Look at each interview panel member when answering each question. Even though an interview question will be asked by one member of the panel at a time, you should always respond to the entire panel collectively. Look them in the eyes when speaking to them but never stare them out. This will only portray you in an aggressive or confrontational manner.

If you are unsure about a response to an interview question then just be honest. Consider saying something along the lines of:

"I am sorry I do not know the answer to that question. I will look the answer up as soon as I get back home and contact you to let you know the answer."

If they accept this response, make sure you do research the response and contact them to let them know.

When the interview panel are speaking to me, or if they are asking me a question, I will always demonstrate good listening skills. This means that I will use facial expressions to show that I am taking on-board what they are saying and I will also nod to show them that I understand the question(s).

BODY LANGUAGE AND POSTURE

Whilst sat in the interview I will always make a conscious effort to sit upright and not slouch in the chair. I personally like to use my hands to emphasise points when responding to the questions but I will be careful not to overdo it. Even if the interview is going great and you are building up a good rapport with the panel, don't let your standards drop. Always maintain good body language and posture for the duration of the interview.

FINAL QUESTIONS

Before I attend the interview I will always think of two questions to ask the panel at the end. However, don't be trapped in the thinking that you must ask questions. It is acceptable to say:

"Thank you but I don't have any questions. I have already carried out lots of research and you have answered some of my questions during the interview."

Some people believe that you must ask three, four or even five questions at the end of the interview – this is total nonsense. Remember that the interview panel will have other people to interview and they will also need time to discuss your performance.

If you do decide to ask questions then make sure they are relevant. Here are a couple of examples:

Q1. Whilst I find out if I am successful or not is there any further literature or books you recommend I read that will further improve my knowledge of the police force and the role of a police special constable?

Q2. I notice that the police force carry out a lot of good work in the community. If I am successful, will I have the opportunity to get involved with the community work once I have passed my initial training and probationary period?

CREATING A POSITIVE FINAL IMPRESSION

A positive final statement can work wonders. Here's an example of what to say:

"I just want to say thank you for inviting me along to interview. I've really enjoyed the experience and I have learnt a tremendous amount

about the role of a police special constable and the good work the force carries out. If I am successful then I promise you that I will work very hard in the role and I will do all that I can to surpass your expectations."

Now move onto the next section of the guide.

INTERVIEW QUESTIONS AND ANSWERS FOR THE POLICE SPECIAL CONSTABLE INTERVIEW

As part of the police special constable assessment centre you will normally be required to sit an interview that is based around the core competencies. Under normal circumstances the interview board will consist of one or two people. These can be from either the uniformed side of the service or support staff.

It is important to remember that whilst you will be nervous you should try not to let this get in the way of your success. Police special constables are confident people who have the ability to rise to a challenge and perform under difficult and pressurised situations. Treat the interview no differently to this. You ARE capable of becoming a police special and the nerves that you have on the day are only natural; in fact they will help you to perform better if you have prepared sufficiently. The crucial element to your success, as with the rest of the selection process, is your preparation.

The police specials interview board will have a number of set questions to choose from and, whilst these are constantly changing, they will usually form part of the police special constable core competencies. Before attending your interview ensure that you read, digest and understand the police special core competencies. Without these it will be difficult to pass the interview.

The interview will last for approximately 20 - 30 minutes depending on the length of your responses. During this time you will be asked a number of questions about specific situations and experiences that are important to the role of the police officer. In relation to the core competency element of the interview there will normally be four questions and you will have just five minutes to answer each of them. Be prepared for additional questions that focus on your reasons and motivations for becoming a police special constable.

These questions will be based around the police officer core competencies and you will be provided with details of these in your information pack, which the police will send you prior to your assessment. The core competencies that are usually assessed at interview are as follows:

- Respect for race and diversity;
- Team working;
- Problem solving;
- Resilience;
- Personal responsibility;
- Customer and community focus;
- Effective communication (not assessed through direct questioning).

In order to ensure you are fully prepared for every eventuality, I will provide you with a sample response to cover every core competency within this section of the guide, with the exception of effective communication. Effective communication is assessed indirectly during the interview.

You will be allowed up to 5 minutes to answer each question so don't be afraid to use the time you have. You may find during the interview that the interviewer asks you probing questions. Probing questions are designed to help you in giving your response so listen to what he or she has to say.

PREPARING FOR THE INTERVIEW

When preparing for the assessment centre competency based interview you should try to formulate responses to questions that surround the assessable core competencies. The responses that you provide should be specific examples of where you have been in that particular scenario.

In your 'welcome pack', which will be sent to you approximately 2 weeks before the date of your assessment centre, you should find examples of the 'core competencies' relevant to a police special constable. These are the criteria that you will be scored against so it is essential you read them beforehand and trying to structure your answers around them as best you can. For example, one of the sections you will be assessed against could be 'Respect for Race and Diversity'. You may be asked a question where you have to give an example of where you have had to respect other people's opinions and views that are from a different culture or background than your own. Try to think of an example where you have had to do this and structure your answer around the core competencies required, e.g. you are respectful to people and treat them with dignity whilst taking into consideration their views and opinions. You are sensitive to language and use it in an appropriate manner etc.

On the following page I have provided you with an example of how your response could be structured if you were responding to a question that was based around the core competency of personal responsibility.

Remember that the following sample question and response is for example purposes only.

SAMPLE INTERVIEW QUESTION BASED AROUND THE CORE COMPETENCY OF PERSONAL RESPONSIBILITY

Q. Please provide an example of where you have taken personal responsibility to arrange or organise an event or situation?

"After reading an appeal in my local paper from a local charity I decided to try to raise money for this worthwhile cause by organising a charity car wash day at the local school during the summer holidays. I decided that the event would take place in a month's time, which would give me enough time to organise such an event.

I set about organising the event and soon realised that I had made a mistake in trying to arrange everything on my own, so I arranged for two of my work colleagues to assist me. Once they had agreed to help I asked one of them to organise the booking of the school and arrange local sponsorship in the form of buckets, sponges and car wash soap to use on the day, so that we did not have to use our own personal money to buy them. I asked the second person to arrange advertising in the local newspaper and radio stations so that we could let the local community know about our charity car wash event, which would in turn hopefully bring in more money on the day for the charity.

Following a successful advertising campaign, I was inundated with calls from local newspapers about our event and it was becoming hard work having to keep talking to them and explaining what the event was all about. But I knew that this information was important if we were to raise our target of £500.

Everything was going well right up to the morning of the event, when I realised we had not got the key to open the school gates. It was the summer holidays so the caretaker was not there to open the gates for us.

Not wanting to let everyone down, I jumped in my car and made my way down to the caretaker's house and managed to wake him up and get the key just in time before the car wash event was due to start. In the end the day was a great success and we all managed to raise £600 for the local charity."

Now that we have taken a look at a sample response, let's explore how the response matched the core competency.

HOW THE RESPONSE MATCHES THE CORE COMPETENCY BEING ASSESSED

In order to demonstrate how effective the above response is we have broken it down into sections and provided the core competency area that it matches.

Sentence

"…I decided to try to raise money for this worthwhile cause by organising a charity car wash day…"

Core competency matched

- Takes on tasks without being asked.
- Uses initiative.

Sentence

"…which would give me enough time to organise such an event."

Core competency matched

- Is conscientious in completing work on time.

Sentence

"I set about organising the event and soon realised that I had made a mistake in trying to arrange everything on my own, so I arranged for 2 of my work colleagues to assist me."

Core competency matched

- Takes responsibility for problems and tasks.
- Takes personal responsibility for own actions.
- Uses initiative.
- Is open, honest and genuine.

Sentence

"…arrange local sponsorship in the form of buckets, sponges and car wash soap to use on the day, so that we did not have to use our own personal money to buy them."

Core competency matched

- Uses initiative.

Sentence

"Following a successful advertising campaign, I was inundated with calls from local newspapers about our event and it was becoming hard work having to keep talking to them and explaining what the event was all about. But I knew that this information was important if we were to raise our target of £500."

Core competency matched

- Focuses on a task even if it is routine.

- Uses initiative.

Sentence

"Not wanting to let everyone down, I jumped in my car and made my way down to the caretaker's house and managed to wake him up and get the key just in time before the car wash event was due to start."

Core competency matched

- Follows things through to a satisfactory conclusion.

- Uses initiative.

- Takes personal responsibility for own actions.

- Keeps promises and does not let colleagues down.

- Takes responsibility for problems and tasks.

The explanations above have hopefully highlighted the importance of matching the core competencies that are being assessed.

When you receive your 'Welcome Pack', make sure you read it thoroughly and prepare yourself fully for the interview. Preparation is everything and by reading exactly what is required you will increase your chances of success on the day.

On the following pages I have provided you with a number of sample assessment centre interview questions that are based around the core competencies. Following each question I have provided you with some useful tips and advice on how you may consider answering the question.

Once you have read the question, the tips and the sample response, use the template provided to create a response using your own experiences and knowledge.

SAMPLE COMPETENCY BASED INTERVIEW QUESTION 2

Q. Please provide an example of where you have worked as part of a team to achieve a difficult task.

Tips for constructing your response

- Try to think of a situation where you volunteered to work with a team in order to achieve a difficult task. It is better to say that you volunteered as opposed to being asked to get involved by another person.

- Those candidates who can provide an example where they achieved the task despite the constraints of time will generally score better.

- Consider structuring your response in the following manner:

STEP 1

Explain what the situation was and how you became involved.

STEP 2

Now explain who else was involved and what the task was.

STEP 3

Explain why the task was difficult and whether there were any time constraints.

STEP 4

Explain how it was decided who would carry out what task.

STEP 5

Now explain what had to be done and how you overcame any obstacles or hurdles.

STEP 6

Explain what the result/outcome was. Try to make the result positive as a result of your actions.

SAMPLE RESPONSE TO COMPETENCY BASED INTERVIEW
QUESTION 2

Q. Please provide an example of where you have worked as part of a team to achieve a difficult task.

"I like to keep fit and healthy and as part of this aim I play hockey for a local Sunday team. We had worked very hard to get to the cup final and we were faced with playing a very good opposition team who had recently won the league title. After only ten minutes of play, one of our players was sent off and we conceded a penalty as a result. Being one goal down and 80 minutes left to play we were faced with a mountain to climb. However, we all remembered our training and worked very hard in order to prevent any more goals being scored. Due to playing with fewer players I had to switch positions and play as a defender, something that I am not used to. However, I understood that the team always comes first and I knuckled down, remembered my training and performed to the best of my ability in the unfamiliar position. The team worked brilliantly to hold off any further opposing goals and after 60 minutes we managed to get an equaliser. The game went to penalties in the end and we managed to win the cup. I believe I am an excellent team player and can always be relied upon to work as an effective team member at all times. I understand that being an effective team member is very important if the police force is to provide a high level of service to the community."

SAMPLE COMPETENCY BASED INTERVIEW QUESTION 3

Q. Provide an example of where you have challenged someone's behaviour that was either discriminatory or inappropriate. What did you do and what did you say?

Tips for constructing your response

- The competency of Respect for Race and Diversity is very important. It is vital you take the time to provide solid evidence of where you meet this area.

- Read carefully the core competency that relates to respect for race and diversity before constructing your response.

- When challenging this type of behaviour, make sure you remain calm at all times and never become aggressive or confrontational.

- Consider structuring your response in the following manner:

STEP 1

Explain what the situation was and how you became involved.

STEP 2

Now explain who else was involved and why you felt that the behaviour was inappropriate or discriminatory. What was it that was being said or done?

STEP 3

Now explain what you said or did and why.

STEP 4

Explain how the other person/people reacted when you challenged the behaviour.

STEP 5

Now explain what the end result was. Try to make the result positive following your actions.

STEP 6

Finally explain why you think it was that the people/person behaved as they did.

SAMPLE RESPONSE COMPETENCY BASED INTERVIEW
QUESTION 3

Q. Provide an example of where you have challenged someone's behaviour that was either discriminatory or inappropriate. What did you do and what did you say?

"I recently worked part-time in a local supermarket. One of my colleagues, a lad called Jamie, had special needs. Jamie was an excellent worker who always gave his all during the working day. He sometimes struggled to remember where certain items of groceries were located in the store, but other than this minor issue his work was outstanding.

One day I overheard a customer being rude to Jamie after he struggled to find an item of food the customer has requested. The customers unfortunate gestures had made him nervous and he started to panic. I immediately made my way over to the situation in order to support Jamie and to try and resolve the situation in a calm manner. I started off by standing next to Jamie and telling him that everything was going to be alright and that I would take over from here. I asked the lady what the problem was. She began to explain in an agitated and slightly aggressive manner that Jamie was 'useless at his job' and that he was an 'idiot' for failing to locate the tomato ketchup for here when she requested his assistance.

I immediately challenged her comments and informed her that these comments would not be tolerated. I asked her to take into consideration the fact that Jamie, whilst an exceptional employee, had special needs. I requested that she refrained from raising her voice and to also take into consideration how her actions had made him feel. I made sure that I was polite, tolerant and patient when dealing with the situation but I also ensured that I took into consideration her offending action and how it was making Jamie feel.

She immediately apologised to Jamie for her lack of understanding and inappropriate words. I then told Jamie where he could find the tomato ketchup and he then took the lady along to find the item for her.

Overall I believe this situation was dealt with in an appropriate and successful manner. I managed to prevent the situation from deteriorating whilst maintaining high levels of customer service."

SAMPLE COMPETENCY BASED INTERVIEW QUESTION 4

Q. Provide an example of where you have helped somebody from a different culture or background to your own. What did you do and what did you say?

Tips for constructing your response

- Read carefully the core competency that relates to respect for race and diversity before constructing your response.

- Try to think of a situation where you have gone out of your way to help somebody.

- Try to use keywords and phrases from the core competency in your response.

- Consider structuring your response in the following manner:

STEP 1

Explain what the situation was and how you became involved. It is better to say that you volunteered to be involved rather than to say that you were asked to.

STEP 2

Now explain who else was involved and why they needed your help or assistance?

STEP 3

Now explain what you said or did and why. Also explain any factors you took into consideration when helping them.

STEP 4

Explain how the other person/people reacted to your help or assistance. Did they benefit from it?

STEP 5

Now explain what the end result was. Try to make the result positive following your actions.

SAMPLE RESPONSE TO COMPETENCY BASED INTERVIEW
QUESTION 4

Q. Provide an example of where you have helped somebody from a different culture or background to your own. What did you do and what did you say?

"I was working at a restaurant and noticed a divide between the waiters and kitchen staff. Most of the kitchen staff were older than their waiter colleagues and had migrated from India. There was very little interaction between the kitchen and waiter staff colleagues and I was concerned that this barrier would not only make the kitchen staff feel isolated, but that it would also have a negative impact on the team environment.

My initial considerations were to ensure that the kitchen staff felt comfortable and that they could also speak to me and the waiters if they needed help or assistance. After all, they had not been in the country for long and I wanted them to feel welcome and valued. I believe that communication between colleagues within a workplace is essential to achieve the best possible results and create a good working environment, regardless of individual differences.

To overcome the challenges I introduced myself to all the kitchen staff members and I learnt their names. This ensured that they felt valued and that they also had a point of contact if they ever needed assistance or support. I also encouraged the other waiters to communicate with their kitchen colleagues. Following my actions communication improved and the workplace is now a more efficient and happier working environment."

SAMPLE COMPETENCY BASED INTERVIEW QUESTION 5

Q. Provide an example of where you have solved a difficult problem. What did you do?

Tips for constructing your response

- Read carefully the core competency that relates to problem solving.
- Try to include keywords and phrases from the core competency in your response to this question.
- Consider structuring your response in the following manner:

STEP 1

Explain what the situation was and why the problem was difficult.

STEP 2

Now explain what action you took in order to solve the difficult problem?

STEP 3

Now explain why you took that particular action, and also the thought process behind your actions.

STEP 4

Explain the barriers or difficulties that you had to overcome?

STEP 5

Now explain what the end result was. Try to make the result positive following your actions.

SAMPLE RESPONSE TO COMPETENCY BASED INTERVIEW
QUESTION 5

Q. Provide an example of where you have solved a difficult problem. What did you do?

"I was working in a retail shop and it was a busy trading day in the run up to Christmas. We had been advertising a promotion for a new brand of perfume in the local press that was due to launch the very next day. All of a sudden a member of staff approached me and informed me that no stock of the new perfume had been delivered and that time had run out to get any delivered before the following days trade commenced. This obviously spelt disaster for the company as many people had placed pre-orders of the new perfume and they would be coming in store to collect their goods.

I started off by calling a meeting of three key members of staff. We gathered in the staff room and I co-ordinated a brain storming session in order to resolve the issue. I started off by gathering as much information as possible. The key facts I gained were:

1. The time we had left in order to get some stock delivered.

2. How much stock we needed to fulfil pre-orders.

3. Who was available to work late that evening?

4. Who had transport and a full driving licence?

Once I had gathered the facts I then developed a plan to resolve the problem. I asked a member of the team to phone around all company stores in the county to establish which shops had extra stock. I then assigned another member of staff who was willing to work late to drive out to the stores in order to borrow the extra surplus stock. I then personally placed an initial order with the distributer so that we had enough stock to fulfil orders for the entire Christmas period and to also pay back the stock we had borrowed from other stores in the County.

The result of the situation was that we managed to obtain sufficient stock to fulfil the orders the next day. Finally, I carried out a full investigation as to why this situation had occurred in the first place with a view to making sure it never happened again."

SAMPLE COMPETENCY BASED INTERVIEW QUESTION 6

Q. Provide an example of where you have completed a task despite pressure from others. What did you do and what did you say?

Tips for constructing your response

- Read carefully the core competency that relates to problem solving.
- Try to include keywords and phrases from the core competency in your response to this question.
- Consider structuring your response in the following manner:

STEP 1

Explain what the situation was and why you were under pressure.

STEP 2

Now explain what steps you took in order to complete the task on time.

STEP 3

Now explain why you took that particular action, and also the thought process behind your actions.

STEP 4

Explain the barriers or difficulties that you had to overcome in order to finish the task on time?

STEP 5

Now explain what the end result was. Try to make the result positive following your actions.

SAMPLE RESPONSE TO COMPETENCY BASED INTERVIEW
QUESTION 6

Q. Provide an example of where you have completed a task despite pressure from others. What did you do and what did you say?

"In my current job as car mechanic for a well-known company I was presented with a difficult and pressurised situation. A member of the team had made a mistake and had fitted a number of wrong components to a car. The car in question was due to be picked up at 2pm and the customer had stated how important it was that his car was ready on time because he had an important meeting to attend.

We only had two hours in which to resolve the issue and I volunteered to be the one who would carry out the work on the car. The problem was that we had three other customers in the workshop waiting for their cars too, so I was the only person who could be spared at that particular time. In order to solve the problem I first of all gathered appropriate information. This included exactly what needed to be done and in what priority. I also established what realistically could be done and what couldn't be done in the time-frame given.

I worked solidly for the next two hours making sure that I meticulously carried out each task in line with our operating procedures. Even though I didn't finish the car until 2.10pm, I managed to achieve all of the tasks under pressurised conditions whilst keeping strictly to procedures and regulations."

SAMPLE COMPETENCY BASED INTERVIEW QUESTION 7

Q. Please provide an example of where you have had to make a difficult decision despite pressure from other people.

Tips for constructing your response

- Read carefully the core competency that relates to resilience.
- Try to include keywords and phrases from the core competency in your response to this question.
- Consider structuring your response in the following manner:

STEP 1

Explain what the situation was and who was involved.

STEP 2

Now explain why the decision was difficult and what pressure you were under.

STEP 3

Now explain what you did and why you did it.

STEP 4

Explain what the other people did or said in reaction to your decision and explain why you think they reacted as they did.

STEP 5

Finally explain what the end result was. Try to provide a positive outcome to the situation.

SAMPLE RESPONSE TO COMPETENCY BASED INTERVIEW
QUESTION 7

Q. Please provide an example of where you have had to make a difficult decision despite pressure from other people.

"My son is in his final year at the local school. To date, his work has been exceptional and every parents evening we attend he is praised by his teachers. However, recently there was an incident that involved very poor judgement on my son's part. He got involved with a group of youths from school who were bullying a boy who was less fortunate than themselves. The matter was brought to my attention by the boy's Father. He contacted me by letter and explained that my son had allegedly been involved in the bullying behaviour with the other youths. I immediately asked my son if the allegations were true. He immediately owned up to his part in the bullying, much to the horror of my wife and I.

I decided that the best course of action was to take my son into school and to make the Head teacher aware of the situation with a view for my son to be punished in line with the schools discipline procedures. My wife totally disagreed with my planned course of action and started to put pressure on me to deal with this within the family environment.

However, I maintained my stance. I was determined that my son should be punished by the school first and foremost. By taking this course of action I believed that my son would learn from his mistake and that he would never carry out this dreadful act again. I also wanted to ensure that the other offending youths were punished by the school too, as this would act as a deterrent to anyone else in the school who was thinking of bullying an individual.

Whilst my wife still disagreed with me to this day I believe the course of action I took was appropriate given the seriousness of the situation. My son was punished by the school and has since maintained a very high level of discipline both at school and at home."

HOW TO IMPROVE YOUR SCORES THROUGH EFFECTIVE COMMUNICATION

I mentioned earlier on in the guide that you will be assessed indirectly by effective communication. I will now provide you with some important tips to help you score high in this competency.

During interview, the panel will be looking to see how you communicate and also how you structure your responses to the interview questions.

Consider the following points both during the interview and whilst responding to the interview questions:

- When you walk into the interview room stand up straight and introduce yourself. Be polite and courteous at all times and try to come across in a pleasant manner. The panel will be assessing you as soon as you walk through the door so make sure you make a positive first impression.

- Do not sit down in the interview chair until you are invited to do so. This is good manners.

- When you sit down in the interview chair, sit up straight and do not fidget or slouch. It is acceptable to use hand gestures when explaining your responses to the questions but don't overdo it, as they can become a distraction.

- Structure your responses to the questions in a logical manner – this is very important. When responding to an interview question, start at the beginning and work your way through in a concise manner, and at a pace that is easy for the panel to listen to.

- Speak clearly and in a tone that is easy for the panel to hear. Be confident in your responses.

- When talking to the panel use eye contact but be careful not to look at them in an intimidating manner.

- Consider wearing some form of formal outfit to the interview such as a suit. Whilst you will not be assessed on the type of outfit you wear to the interview, it will make you come across in a more professional manner.

FINAL GOLDEN INTERVIEW TIPS

- Always provide 'specific' examples to the questions being asked.

- During your responses try to outline your contributions and also provide evidence of the competency area that is being assessed.

- Speak clearly, use correct English and structure their responses in a logical and concise manner.

FURTHER INTERVIEW QUESTIONS AND ANSWERS FOR THE POLICE SPECIAL CONSTABLE INTERVIEW

Within this section of the guide I have provided you with further insider tips and advice on how to prepare for the interview, the type of questions that you may be asked in addition to the core competency questions and also how to respond to them. I have also provided you with space after many of the questions in which I would like you to formulate your own response based on your experiences and research. This will be excellent practice for the interview so please take the time to construct your own answers.

To begin with, let's take a look at a few more details about how you can get the most from your preparation.

INTERVIEW TECHNIQUE

Many candidates spend little or no time improving or developing their interview technique. It is important that you spend sufficient time on this area, as it will allow your confidence to improve.

The way to improve interview technique is to carry out what we call a mock interview. Mock interviews are where you ask a friend or relative to ask you a number of interview questions under formalised interview conditions. This can be achieved at home across your dining room table or even whilst sat on the chairs in your living room.

During the mock interview you should work on your interview technique. The mock interview will also give you a valuable opportunity to try out your responses to a number of sample interview questions that are contained within this guide. It is important that your mock interviewer provides you with constructive feedback. Do not choose somebody who will tell you that you were great, even when you weren't, as this just defeats the whole purpose of a mock interview.

CARRYING OUT A MOCK INTERVIEW

- Choose a quiet room in the house or at another suitable location.

- Set the room up with a table and two chairs.

- The interviewer then invites you into the room and the interview commences. Don't forget to be polite and courteous to the interviewer and only sit down when invited to do so.

- When the interviewer asks you the questions, respond to them in a logical manner and in a tone of voice that can be easily heard.

- Throughout the mock interview work hard on your technique and style. Sit upright at all times and look at the interviewer using soft eye contact. Do not fidget or slouch in the interview chair.

- Once the interview is over, ask the interviewer for feedback on your performance.

- Repeat the process at least three times until you are comfortable with your technique and style of answering.

THE REASONS WHY YOU WANT TO BECOME A POLICE SPECIAL CONSTABLE AND WHAT YOU KNOW ABOUT THE ROLE

During the interview the panel may ask you questions that relate to why you want to become a police special constable and in particular what you know about the role.

WHY DO YOU WANT TO BECOME A POLICE SPECIAL CONSTABLE?

In the build-up to your interview you need to think carefully about why you want to become a police special and what it is exactly that has attracted you to the role. Remember, it is a voluntary role, so you will need to have good reasons why you want join the force.

Those candidates who want to become a police special so that they can 'catch criminals' and 'ride about in a police car with the blue lights flashing' will score poorly. Only you will know the exact reasons why you want to join the police as a special but here are some examples of good reasons, and examples of poor reasons.

Good reasons to give

- To make a difference to your community, make it a safer place and reduce any fear that the public may have.
- To carry out a job that is worthwhile and one that makes a difference.
- The variety of the job and the different challenges that you will face on a day-to-day basis.
- The chance to work with a highly professional team that is committed to achieving the values and principles of the force.
- The opportunity to learn new skills.

Poor reasons to give

- Wearing a uniform, which ultimately means you don't have to pay for your own work clothes.
- Catching criminals and driving a police car.

WHAT DO YOU KNOW ABOUT THE ROLE?

Before the interview you must carry out plenty of research into the role and what the force will expect of you as a serving police special constable.

Remember that the role is predominantly based around the core competencies, so be fully familiar with them before you attend the interview. It is also advisable that you study the police recruitment website, your recruitment literature, and also the website of the force you are applying to join.

APPLICATION FORM

During the interview the panel may ask you questions that relate to your application form. Before you attend the final interview familiarise yourself with the contents of your form and be prepared for any questions that you may be asked relating to it.

WHAT YOU KNOW ABOUT THE FORCE YOU ARE APPLYING TO JOIN

During the interview there is a possibility that you will be asked questions that relate to the force you are applying to join.

The following sample questions are the types that have been asked during final interviews in the past:

Q. What is it that has attracted you to this particular force?

Have a good understanding of your local community and the problems that it faces. I also recommend you visit the website of the force you are applying to join. Find out what pro-active measures they are taking in their fight against crime and use it in your response. Here's a good response to this question:

"Having lived in the county for many years I am already familiar with the good work the force carries out. I am constantly reading about the good news stories the police are carrying out in the local community and I want to be part of the organisation. Not only am I impressed with the local, pro-active initiatives that are being carried out but I am also want to be a part of an organisation that cares about the work it does. During my research I also noticed that the force encourages members of the public to talk online

to their local police officer's and specials. I think this is a fantastic way of encouraging the local community to build relationships with the police, as this in turn builds trust and enables the officers to gather intelligence and vital information in their work against crime in the community."

Q. What can you tell me about the structure of this force?

Visit the force's website to find out more about the structure and make-up of the organisation you are wishing to join.

Q. What can you tell me about the geographical area of this police force?

You can find out this information by spending time on the police force website. In addition to this there is also nothing to stop you from visiting your local police station and requesting information on the geographical layout of the force. The best people to gain this information from are your local police officers, police specials and police community support officers.

Q. Can you tell me how this force is doing in relation to crime reduction?

You can find out this information on the forces website. A word of warning though, if the force is not doing particularly well in a specific area do not repeat any negative press stories during the interview. Always focus on the positive work they are doing. For example, whenever I was interviewed by the television cameras immediately following a fire, I would always put a positive spin on the story. If we had lost 80% of the building to fire, I would never actually state this during the television interview. Instead, I would say something like:

"Fire crews worked extremely hard throughout the night to fight the fire. They carried out some excellent work and they managed to save 20% of the building."

This sounds much better than saying we lost 80%!

Q. What crime reduction activities is this force currently involved in?

Again, you can find this out on the forces website. I would also recommend visiting:

WWW.POLICE.UK

Q. What is neighbourhood policing and how does this force approach it?

Neighbourhood Policing is provided by teams of police officers, police specials and Police Community Support Officers (PCSOs) in each individual force, often together with local authority wardens, volunteers and partners. There are now 3,600 Neighbourhood Policing Teams (NPTs) across the UK. Local Policing aims to provide people who live or work in a neighbourhood with:

Access — to local policing services through a named point of contact

Influence — over policing priorities in their neighbourhood

Interventions — joint action with partners & the public

Answers — sustainable solutions & feedback on what is being done

This means that neighbourhood teams:

- publicise how to get in touch with them
- find out what the local issues are that make people feel unsafe in their neighbourhood and ask them to put them in order of priority
- decide with partners and local people what should be done to deal with those priorities and work with them to deliver the solutions
- let people know what is being done and find out if they are satisfied with the results.

Q. What are the ambitions of this police force?

You can find out this information on the website of the force you are applying to join. For example, my local police force is Kent. On their website they publish a 3 year plan which sets out their plans and objectives for the forthcoming 3 yearly period. At the time of writing, their plans include:

Priorities	Objectives
Delivering effective local policing	Reducing crime and effectively dealing with anti-social behaviour;
	Improving visibility, accessibility and responsiveness;
	Improving public satisfaction;
	Bringing offenders to justice.
Protecting the public from serious harm	Protecting the public from serious and organised crime.
Making best use of our resources	Demonstrating increasing efficiency and value for money.

Q. Who are our partners and stakeholders?

In general, the stakeholders and partners of the police include:

- Communities within the police force area, including those who are not resident but work or travel within the county.
- Police Authority; Government Office for the area, MEPs, MPs, Independent Advisory Groups; Special Interest Groups, County, Borough/District councils/councillors; Community Safety Partnerships; Local Criminal Justice Board; Unions and Staff Associations; County/Regional media organisations; 3rd party organisations; Neighbourhood Watch and Business Watch.
- Fire and Rescue Service, Ambulance Service, Local Authority, Coastguard, CCTV groups, Environmental Agency.
- Police staff, Police officers, Specials, SPOCs and volunteers.

In order to prepare for questions that relate to the force you are applying to join, your first port of call is their website. From here you will be able to find out a considerable amount of information about their structure and activities, including the policing pledge and their success in driving down crime.

You may also wish to consider contacting your local police station and asking if it is possible to talk to a serving police officer about his or her role and the activities that the force are currently engaged in.

SITUATIONAL INTERVIEW QUESTIONS

During the interview the panel may ask you questions that relate to how you would respond or act in a given situation. This type of question is called a 'situational' type question.

Your response to each situational question must be 'specific' in nature. This means that you must provide an example where you have already been in this type of situation. During your response you should provide details of how you handled or dealt with the situation, preferably with a successful outcome.

Do not fall into the trap of providing a 'generic' response that details what you 'would do' if the situation arose, unless of course you have not been in this type of situation before.

When responding to situational questions try to structure your responses in a logical and concise manner. The way to achieve this is to use the 'STAR' method of interview question response construction:

Situation

Start off your response to the interview question by explaining what the 'situation' was and who was involved.

Task

Once you have detailed the situation, explain what the 'task' was, or what needed to be done.

Action

Now explain what 'action' you took, and what action others took. Also explain why you took this particular course of action.

Result

Explain what the outcome or result was following your actions and those of others. Try to demonstrate in your response that the result was positive because of the action you took.

Finally, explain to the panel what you would do differently if the same situation arose again. It is good to be reflective at the end of your responses. This demonstrates a level of maturity and it will also show the panel that you are willing to learn from every experience.

Now that we have looked into how to prepare for the interview, it is time to provide you with a number of sample questions and answers. Please note that the questions provided here are for practice purposes only and are not to be relied upon to be the exact questions that you will be asked during your interview. I cannot guarantee that these questions will form part of the police specials interview. However, if you want to be 100% prepared, I recommend you prepare for them. I have provided you with space after each question to write down your own notes and response to the question.

SAMPLE INTERVIEW QUESTIONS AND SAMPLE RESPONSES

SAMPLE QUESTION NUMBER 1

Q. Tell us why you want to become a police special constable?

SAMPLE RESPONSE

"I have worked in my current role now for a number of years. I have an excellent employer and enjoy working for them but unfortunately no longer find my job challenging. I understand that the role of a police special is both demanding and rewarding and I believe I have the qualities to thrive in such an environment. I love working under pressure, working as part of a team that is diverse in nature and helping people in difficult situations. The public expectations of the police are very high and I believe I have the right qualities to help the police deliver the right service to the community.

I have studied the police special constable core competencies and believe that I have the skills to match them and deliver what they require."

Top tips

- Don't be negative about your current or previous employer.
- Be positive, enthusiastic and upbeat in your response.
- Make reference to the core competencies if possible.

NOTES:

SAMPLE QUESTION NUMBER 2

Q. Why have you chosen this particular Police Force?

SAMPLE RESPONSE

"I have carried out extensive research into the Police Service and in particular this force. I have been impressed by the level of service it provides. The website provides the community with direct access to a different range of topics and the work that is being carried out through your community wardens is impressive. I have looked at the national and local crime statistics and read many different newspapers and articles.

I like this Police Force because of its reputation and the police officers and specials that I have spoken to have told me that they get a great deal of job satisfaction from working here."

Top tips

- Research the force thoroughly and make reference to particular success stories that they have achieved.

- Be positive, enthusiastic and upbeat in your response.

- Be positive about their force and don't be critical of it, even if you think it needs improving in certain areas.

NOTES:

SAMPLE QUESTION NUMBER 3

Q. What does the role of a police special constable involve?

SAMPLE RESPONSE

"Before I carried out my research and looked into the role of the police special constable, I had the normal, stereotypical view in that they catch criminals and reduce crime for a living.

Whilst there is an element of that in the job, the police specials role is far more diverse and varied. For example, they are there to serve the community and reduce the element of fear. They do this by communicating with their communities and being visual wherever possible. Their role is to also to help regular police officers protect the community.

They may need to pay particular attention to a person or groups of people who are the victims of crime or hatred. Therefore the role of a police special is to both physically and psychologically protect the community that they are serving.

It is also their role to work with other organisations such as the Fire Service, Social Services and other public sector bodies to try to reduce crime in a coordinated response as opposed to on their own."

Top tips

- Understand the police special core competencies and be able to recite them word for word.

- Understand the term 'community policing'.

NOTES:

SAMPLE QUESTION NUMBER 4

Q. If one of the members of your team was gay and they told you this over a cup of tea at work, how do you think you would react?

SAMPLE RESPONSE

"I would have no problem at all. A person's sexual preference is their right and they should not be treated any differently for this. My attitude towards them and our working relationship would not be affected in any way. I have always treated everyone with respect and dignity at all times and will continue to do so throughout my career."

Top tips

- Understand everything there is to know about equality and fairness. If you do not believe in it then this job is not for you.

- Visit the website www.gay.police.uk

NOTES:

SAMPLE QUESTION NUMBER 5

Q. If you were given an order that you thought was incorrect would you carry it out?

SAMPLE RESPONSE

"Yes I would. I would always respect my senior officers and their decisions.

However, if I thought something could be done in a better way, then I do think that it is important to put it across but in a structured and non-confrontational manner. During a debrief would probably be an appropriate time to offer up my views and opinions if asked but I would never refuse to carry out an order or even question it during an operational incident or otherwise."

Top tips

- It is good to say that you would offer suggestions.
- The police force is a disciplined environment; therefore, you will be expected to carry out orders without question.

NOTES:

SAMPLE QUESTION NUMBER 6

Q. What do you understand by the term equality and fairness?

SAMPLE RESPONSE

"It is an unfortunate fact that certain groups in society are still more likely to suffer from unfair treatment and discrimination. It is important for the Police Force and its staff to strive to eliminate all forms of unfair treatment and discrimination on the grounds that are specified in their policies or codes of practice. Equality and fairness is the working culture in which fair treatment of all is the norm."

Top tips

- Try to read the Police Force's policy on equality and fairness. You may be able to find this by visiting their website or asking them for a copy of it to help you in your preparation.

- Consider reading the Race Relations Act, and understand the duties that are placed upon public sector organisations such as the police.

NOTES:

SAMPLE QUESTION NUMBER 7

Q. How do you think the police could recruit more people from minority groups?

SAMPLE RESPONSE

"To begin with it is important that Police Forces continue to build effective public relations. This can be achieved through certain avenues such as the force's website or even the local press. If the Police Force has a community liaison officer then this would be a good way to break down any barriers in the communities that we want to recruit from.

Another option is to ask people from these specific groups how they view this Police Force and what they think we could do to recruit more people from their community. Along with this it may be an option to focus media campaigns where there are higher populations of ethnic minority groups."

Top tips

- Have a good knowledge of the police forces equality policy.
- Try and com e up with your own ideas for recruiting diverse members of the community.

NOTES:

MORE POLICE OFFICER INTERVIEW QUESTIONS TO PREPARE FOR AND TIPS HOW TO RESPOND

Q. Why do you want to become a police special constable?

Remember to include in your response things like:

- Having the ability to improve society through pro-active police work
- Protecting the public
- Making a positive difference to the community
- Using your skills and attributes in a positive manner
- The challenge that comes with the role
- Being part of a disciplined and successful organisation
- Being in an organisation where the opportunity for development exists

NOTES:

Q. What are your strengths?

Try and provide strengths which are relevant to the role and the core competencies being assessed. The following list contains some recommendations:

- Driven, motivated and enthusiastic
- Determined and persistent
- Organised and capable of keeping an accurate and up-to-date diary
- Mentally and physically fit
- Punctual and reliable
- Able to take, keep and record accurate notes
- Flexible and happy to work shifts/unsociable hours
- Able to identify my weak areas and take steps to improve them
- Always looking for ways to develop and improve
- Calm in a crisis
- Able to work alone and unsupervised
- An ability to defuse difficult situations
- A good listener and communicator
- A great team-worker and someone who fits in well to any team
- A hard worker

NOTES:

Q. What are your weaknesses?

This question is harder to respond to than the previous one. Here's a sample response to help you:

"I don't have many weaknesses but those that I do have I am aware of and I am taking steps to improve. During the selection process for becoming a police special I found it difficult to carry out the tests that form part of the initial recruitment test. This is because it has been a long time since I was in education. However, in order to improve in this weak area I started attending night school in order to get some much-needed tuition. I always try to improve on my weaknesses, whatever they are."

NOTES:

Q. What can you tell us about this particular Police Force?

The following sample response is based on Greater Manchester Police Force at the time of writing:

"Greater Manchester Police was formed in 1974 and it now serves more than 2.5 million people. The approximate area it covers is 500 square miles. The police force is divided into twelve divisions, which are Bolton, Bury, Metropolitan, North Manchester, Oldham, Rochdale, Salford, South Manchester, Stockport, Tameside, Trafford and Wigan. There is also a specialist division based at Manchester International Airport. The main objectives of the force are to carry out effective policing by putting people first in everything they do, being proud of delivering excellent service, working with, and for, the people of Greater Manchester in order to make communities safe and feel safer. Neighbourhood Policing is at the heart of Greater Manchester Police. The main aim is to make Greater Manchester a better place to live, work and play. The force prides itself on having the right people in the right place at the right time, tackling everything from anti-social behaviour and burglary to terrorism and organised crime. During my research I have found out that Greater Manchester each of the twelve divisions has a combination of Neighbourhood Policing Units, each of which is managed by a Neighbourhood Inspector. These units have specific areas of responsibility and consist of smaller, localised, Neighbourhood Policing Teams which include local police officers and Police Community Support Officers. These Neighbourhood Policing Teams have been set up to focus on the needs of the local community. They have regular meetings where members of the public can help set the priorities for their area."

NOTES:

Q. What do you understand by the term 'teamwork'?

"In general terms teamwork is the process of working collaboratively with a group of people in order to achieve a goal. Teamwork is often a crucial part of an organisation, as it is often necessary for colleagues to work well together, trying their best in any circumstance. Teamwork means that people will try to cooperate, using their individual skills and providing constructive feedback, despite any personal conflict between individuals. In respect of teamwork in the police force the same applies. Everyone who works in, or for, the police force will work towards the mission and objectives that the force dictates. Within the police force there will be many team members, including call handling staff, police officers, senior managers, police special constables, PCSOs to name just a few. Even the cleaners who maintain the cleanliness of the police stations are an integral part of the team."

NOTES:

Q. What qualities should a team member have?

There are basically a number of qualities that an individual should have in order to become a competent team member. Here are just a few:

- An ability to work towards the aims and objectives of the team
- An ability to support other team members
- An excellent communicator
- Strength of mind
- Sense of humour
- Reliability
- An ability to listen
- Able to contribute towards the team
- Creativity
- Problem solver
- Respectful of the other team members
- An ability to work with everyone, regardless of who they are or their background

NOTES:

Q. Why would you make a good police special constable?

Here's a sample response to this question:

"I believe I would make a good police special constable because I have a desire to work within the community and also work towards making it a safer place to live, work and play. I have some great qualities that I believe would help the police force deliver its objectives. To begin with, I always remain calm in a crisis situation and have a confident and resilient approach to my work, whatever it may be. I have a track record for working hard and I have a flexible nature. I also have some experience of working unsociable hours so I know that this part of the job will not be a problem to me. I also have exceptional organisational skills and can be relied upon to keep accurate records whenever required. Finally I am a very good team worker and enjoy working with people from different backgrounds."

NOTES:

Q. If you saw a colleague being bullied or harassed, what would you do?

No form of bullying or harassment should ever be tolerated, not only in the workplace but also in the community. Here's a sample response to assist you during your preparation:

"The first thing I would do is intervene and stop it. I strongly believe that there is no place in the workplace and society for bullying or harassment. I would remain calm and intervene without physical force or aggression. If necessary, I would try and act as a mediator between the two parties with a view to resolving the issue. If I believed that either party were in serious danger then I would report the incident to my line manager immediately."

NOTES:

Q. What do you think the qualities of an effective police special constable are?

"I believe the qualities include trust, determination, integrity, reliability, being community-focused, a great team-worker, a good communicator, caring, resilient, confident, physically and mentally fit, organised, punctual, an ability to keep accurate notes and records and also being a positive role model."

NOTES:

Q. What have you done so far to find out about the role of a police special?

"I have spent lots of time learning and understanding the core competencies that are relevant to the role. I did this because I wanted to be fully 100% sure that I could carry out the role, and I believe that I can. I have spent time studying the police force website in order to learn about the geographical area and also how the force interacts with the members of the community in which it serves. I have also studied the three year community plan that the force has published. It was important for me to read this document as I understand that I would have to work towards these important goals if I am to be successful. I have also visited my local police station and spent time talking to the local officers about their work. Finally, I attended a local neighbourhood watch meeting in my parish area. This was a great insight into the work the force carries out. I now fully understand how committed the police force is to improving the community."

NOTES:

Q. Give an example of when you have had to work as a team.

"I have had lots of experience to date working as part of a team. In my current role as a bricklayer I have been working on a project with many other skilled workers and labourers. The project involves building ten new houses within a three-month period. We are now half way through the project and it is running smoothly and on-time.

During this particular project I have been required to work with people who I did not know before the start of the build. This has not been a problem for me as I have not issue with working with anyone, regardless of who they are. I always start off by introducing myself to the rest of the team and ask the other team-members to introduce themselves. This acts as a bit of an ice-breaker and it gets everyone talking. At the start of each working day we listen carefully to the brief provided by the foreman. As we work through the tasks set by the foreman we communicate with each other clearly so that everyone knows what is going on and whereabouts we all are with the project. If anyone in the building team starts to slow up we all gather round to help them catch up. As a team member I am always focused on the end goal and work very hard to carry out my job meticulously and diligently."

NOTES:

Q. What would you do if a member of your team was not pulling their weight or doing their job effectively?

"I would first of all ask them if there was anything wrong, or if there was anything I could do to support them. The member of the team might be having personal issues, and if this was the case, I would want to support them and help them through it. If it was simply a case of them being lazy, then I would take action to stop it. I would take them to one side and tactfully point out to them how important their role was within the team. I would inform them that without their full attention on the task in hand we would not be able to achieve our goal."

NOTES:

Q. Have you ever had to diffuse a confrontational situation? What did you do and what did you say?

Before creating a response to this question, consider the following:

1. One of the core competencies is that of resilience. You must be capable of defusing confrontational situations in a calm and confident manner.

2. When dealing with this type of situation you should never become confrontational or aggressive yourself.

Now take a look at the following sample response to the question:

"Yes I have, on a number of occasions. Whilst working in my current role as a shop manager I had to defuse a confrontational situation with an angry customer. The customer was not happy with the service he had received and he wanted to complain. I started listening to his concerns, but as he progressed with his complaint, he became angrier and confrontational to the point that I had to intervene. Whilst listening to him I detected that his voice was becoming more aggressive. I very calmly and politely intervened. I asked him to cease from using threatening language and explained to him that I was here to help him but that I would not tolerate abusive language. I also asked him to come to the rear of the shop so that we would be out of the way of the other customers. When we arrived at the rear of the shop I quietly explained that I understood his concerns and that I would do all that I could to resolve them, but in return he had to remain calm and not become confrontational. My approach worked. He apologised for his actions and carried on detailing his complaint in a calm manner. I believe it is important to be calm, yet firm when dealing with situations of this nature."

NOTES:

Q. What are the main issues affecting the police at this current time?

This question is designed to see how up-to-date you are with current affairs and issues affecting the police force in your area. The following sample response is relevant at the time of writing.

"The main issue affecting the police force at present is the restriction is budget that I understand has been placed by the Local Authority. This means the police force must work harder to deliver efficiency savings and therefore make the service better value for money. This may mean that police officers will be required to carry out extra duties, but ultimately, they will need to work more efficiently. Other issues affecting the police include the constant drive to reduce crime in the local area and to make the community a safer place to live, work and play."

NOTES:

Q. What do you understand about the term 'equality and diversity'?

Equality is the current term for 'Equal Opportunities'. It is based on the legal obligation to comply with anti-discrimination legislation. Equality protects people from being discriminated against on the grounds of group membership i.e. sex, race disability, sexual orientation, religion, belief, or age.

Diversity implies a wide range of conditions and characteristics. In terms of organisations and their workforces it is about valuing and reaping the benefits of a varied workforce that makes the best of people's talents whatever their backgrounds.

Diversity encompasses visible and non-visible individual differences. It can be seen in the makeup of your workforce in terms of gender, ethnic minorities, disabled people etc., about where those people are in terms of management positions, job opportunities, terms and conditions in the workplace. Diversity is about respecting individual differences, and people's differences can be many and varied:

- Race
- Culture
- National origin
- Region
- Gender
- Sexual Orientation
- Age
- Marital Status
- Politics
- Religion
- Ethnicity
- Disability
- Socio-economic differences
- Family structure
- Health
- Values

Embracing equality and diversity brings to an organisation a wide range of experience, ideas and creativity whilst giving the individual employee a feeling of being enabled to work to their full potential.

Combined together, equality and diversity drive an organisation to comply with anti-discrimination legislation as well as emphasising the positive benefits of diversity such as drawing on a wider pool of talent, positively motivating all employees and meeting the needs of a wider customer base.

Employers such as the police force are now encouraged to deepen and enrich their "equal opportunities" policies and strategies into an encompassing Equality and Diversity policy with a strategy and action plans that managers, workers and other stakeholders can contribute to and benefit from.

NOTES:

Q. If you ever heard a racist or sexist remark at work, what would you do?

"I would stop it immediately. No form of abuse should be tolerated. I would intervene in a safe and calm manner. I would also ensure that this behaviour was reported to my line manager so that further action could be considered."

NOTES:

Q. How do you think you would cope with working the police shift system?

Working unsociable hours is part and parcel of life in the police force. I worked shifts in the Fire Service for 17 years and it can take its toll after a while. You need to be 100% certain that you can cope with the irregular shift patterns and that your family supports you. Take a look at the following sample response:

"I believe I would cope very well. I have taken into consideration the fact that I would be required to work unsociable hours and I am prepared for this. I have discussed it with my family and I have their full support. I have worked office based hours for many years now and I am actually looking forward to the change."

NOTES:

FINAL TIPS AND ADVICE FOR PREPARING FOR THE INTERVIEW

- The Police may ask you more generic questions relating to your past experiences or skills. These may be in relation to solving problems, working as an effective team member, dealing with difficult or aggressive people and diffusing confrontational situations. Make sure you have examples for each of these.

- Try to speak to current serving police officers and specials of the force that you are applying to join. Ask them what it is like to work for that particular force and what the current policing issues are. From their feedback take the positive points but don't use any detrimental or negative feedback during the interview.

- Try to think of a time when you have made a mistake and how you learnt from the experience. It is always good to say that you 'reflect' on your actions and take necessary steps to improve for next time.

- When you complete the application form make sure you keep a copy of it. Before you go to your interview ensure that you read the application form over and over again as you may find you are asked questions about your responses.

- Don't be afraid to ask the interviewer to repeat a question if you do not hear it the first time. Take your time when answering and be measured in your responses.

- If you don't know the answer to a question then be honest and just say 'I don't know'. This is far better than trying to answer a question that you have no knowledge about. Conversely, if your answer to a question is challenged there is nothing wrong with sticking to your point but make sure you acknowledge the interviewer's thoughts or views. Be polite and never get into a debate.

- You will be scored against the current police core competencies so make sure you try to structure your answers accordingly. The police core competencies are the first thing you should learn during your preparation.

how2become

Visit www.how2become.co.uk to find more titles and courses that will help you to pass the police officer selection process:

- Online police officer testing
- 1-day police officer training course
- Police officer books and DVD's
- Psychometric testing books and CDs

www.how2become.co.uk